ASPoetry

by the same author

Friendships
The Aspie Way
Wendy Lawson
Foreword by Emma Wall
ISBN 978 1 84310 427 8

Sex, Sexuality and the Autism Spectrum
Wendy Lawson
Foreword by Glenys Jones
ISBN 978 1 84310 284 7

Build Your Own Life
A Self-Help Guide For Individuals With Asperger Syndrome
Wendy Lawson
Foreword by Dr Dinah Murray
ISBN 978 1 84310 114 7

Understanding and Working with the Spectrum of Autism
An Insider's View
Wendy Lawson
Foreword by Margot Prior
ISBN 978 1 85302 971 7

Life Behind Glass
A Personal Account of Autism Spectrum Disorder
Wendy Lawson
Foreword by Patricia Howlin
ISBN 978 1 85302 911 0

of related interest

Coming Out Asperger
Diagnosis, Disclosure and Self-Confidence
Edited by Dinah Murray
ISBN 978 1 84310 240 3

ASPoetry

Illustrated Poems from an Aspie Life

Wendy Lawson

Illustrated by Alice Blaes Calder

Jessica Kingsley Publishers
London and Philadelphia

First published in 2006
by Jessica Kingsley Publishers
116 Pentonville Road
London N1 9JB, UK
and
400 Market Street, Suite 400
Philadelphia, PA 19106, USA

www.jkp.com

Library of Congress Cataloging in Publication Data
Lawson, Wendy, 1952-
   ASPoetry : illustrated poems from an aspie life / Wendy Lawson ; illustrated by Alice Blaes
Calder.
      p. cm.
   ISBN-13: 978-1-84310-418-6 (pbk. : alk. paper)
   ISBN-10: 1-84310-418-0 (pbk. : alk. paper) 1. Asperger's syndrome--Patients--Poetry.
2. Autism--Patients--Poetry. I. Title: AS poetry. II. Calder, Alice Blaes. III. Title.
   PS3612.A955A75 2006
   811'.6--dc22

                                   2005034524

British Library Cataloguing in Publication Data
A CIP catalogue record for this book is available from the British Library

ISBN 978 1 84310 418 6

Printed and bound in Great Britain by
MPG Books Group, Cornwall

Contents

Acknowledgements

I want to say thank you to my family and friends for providing access to many of the life experiences I've had; without you I might not have had a reason to write. To all of those strangers who crossed my path, however briefly, for giving me glimpses into fleeting moments of another's life. To life itself for laying claim to me and to Mother Nature; the truest reflection of the changing world of oneself. For being human, alive and autistic, I am grateful.

Introduction

For some of us, poetry might seem a form of written expression that we were made to 'rehearse' as part of some school curriculum or homework requirement. Maybe our experience with poetry was a difficult one, and one that did not make much sense to us. This short book of poetry is a reflection on some of the life experiences that I have travelled through and, as such, depicts a journey that some will be able to relate to. It is not a book full of complicated sentences and abstracts that don't relate to human reality, but a book that expresses many of the common emotions and experiences associated with being human.

I have written poetry since I was able to write. At times my thoughts are in rhyme. Some of the poetry included in this book was written by me as a young child, some of it as a teenager. Most of it was written as an adult. I have tried to illustrate some of my thinking and much of my experience. Of course it is risky to do this, but then I'm a risk taker.

For me, poetry is the best way to connect with the emotive experiences associated with everyday life. My autism means being a bit slower in making connections. When I don't understand something I can write a poem about it. Sometimes the poem opens the door to my understanding. When I'm lost and feeling trapped, sometimes poetry helps me find direction again. When I feel ecstatic and need to express my joy, poetry takes me there. Although I cannot always solve all of my problems through writing about them, I can at least find a form of written expression that helps me relate to them.

Learning that some difficulties are not solvable, but can be livable, has helped me deal with some of my anxieties. I still wish I could dissolve all of the situations that I find problematic but, even if I can't, at least I can accept that life may be less than perfect, and it's OK. I may be less than perfect, but I'm OK. At times I don't feel comfortable, but maybe I need to learn to live with discomfort too, and not always try to make things comfortable. At times I feel sad, bad, angry, upset and/or disappointed. All of these emotions can occur and they are all OK. I'd like for them not to happen, but they won't end my life; they just last for a season then they go away. I can live with this.

It is my hope that you will enjoy this book. Maybe you will identify with parts of it, maybe it will help to illuminate and enrich your understanding of autism. Either way, I wish you a life that is full of promise and fulfilment. Life is like a poem; sometimes it rhymes and sometimes it does not. I guess we each have to find our own mountain among the valleys that surround us. Does your mountain give you clear views and allow you to breathe in clean air? If your current mountain fails to do this you can wait for the weather to change, or you can change mountains.

Childhood

The following poem depicts my birth. Moving out of the familiar and into the unknown is uncomfortable for most of us. In many ways each of us is experiencing 'being born' every time we wake from a big sleep or step into a new adventure. Taking risks is part of life; without them we may never know the fullest meaning of life. The other poetry in this section seeks to depict various portals of autistic experience... Growing up takes time for everyone, but I think it takes us longer.

The Journey of Life

Here in my watery existence life seems calm, muffled and
     buffered.
I like it here.
What is this? I'm being pushed! I'm being forced; I'm being
     suffocated.
I don't like this!
Rough, cold and separated. My life cord is cut.
Home, warm and welcoming, all her doors are shut.
This air I breathe feels jagged and strange,
My throat is dry and raw.
But I remember the watery sounds when Life was arranged,
When all around me was all that I saw.
I liked it then.

This strange and forbidding place begs me stay awhile.
There, surrounding me, the voices offer a smile.
At first I push away from them, too strange and scary for me.
Then I accept, unwillingly, that they will help me see.

Learning to trust and feel safe again, what a journey is this.
Up hill and down dale. Along busy roads. In clear air and
     mists.
Sometimes the road is clearly marked. I know where it will
     lead.

At other times, though, the darkness stays and yet I must
    proceed.
I don't like this.
I want all to be predictable again, just as it all once was.
I may have to accept that this cannot be,
I may have to accept that I cannot be free.
But all is not lost, life still can be; I still can be.
They cannot take this away from me.
I like this.

Each new day comes to us with its delights and demands. It will involve all kinds of change and this will mean transition. It's not just the dramatic changes that influence who we are and what we become, but also the little things we choose and tolerate. Transition can be very uncomfortable, especially if you are unsure if there is anything after or other than what you have known.

Transition

Autism is: 'I like it here, please do let me stay.'
Autism is: 'I know it here, please don't take me away.'
If and when I leave this place to travel to another space,
I need to know it right away. I need to know that I'm OK.
Transition is so fleeting, it leaves not time to stay.
Will I have time to settle, or will I be whisked away?
I know that change can happen.
I know it can take time.
But how can I know what this will mean?
What this will mean for mine.
Transition is about moving, 'to where or what,' one asks?
This is my very question, from present or the past.
Time for me is all the same,
I know not of its future.
I only know I trust in 'now'…tomorrow can come; I just need
    to know how.

As a child growing up I was expected to 'play' with other children. For me, the difficulty was that I didn't have a concept of what play was or why it was considered to be fun. Most children's play made no sense to me. On reflection I think it might have done if children had been encouraged to join my world at times and if I had felt they were interested in me.

What is Play?

'Wendy, Wendy,' I hear the teacher say.
'Wendy, Wendy, please look this way.'
'Wendy, Wendy,' I hear the children say.
'Wendy, Wendy, please come and play.'

I hear the words that come each day,
'What do they mean?' I hear me say.
Words without pictures simply go away.
I turn my head and look instead
At all that glitters; blue, green and red.

'You'll like it here,' Father speaks,
'Come and play with Billy.'
Inside my head my brain just freaks,
'How can they be so silly?'

'Why would I want to do this thing?'
My mind can find no reason.
'Please leave me with the sparkly string,
This gives me such a feeling.'

The following poem was written as an adult, but reflects upon the feelings I had as an older child. I felt alienated from the world around me and quite perplexed by the complexities of relationships.

Please Accept Me

I'm not the same on the outside as I am on the inside. I smile, I laugh, but I don't know joy. Where is my joy? I try to watch from a safe distance, but nothing seems safe. I used to feel a sense of freedom. I could flick my fingers in front of my face to make the scenery change, like many still pictures become a film when flicked through quickly. This action creates a sense of movement while keeping still. When it was only me no one else mattered; it was as if they did not exist. Everything was once so free. Once grass was green and hills were inviting. Now they are covered with mist and veiled in smog. The greyness forbids me. What was once clear is now murky and unsure.

Inside is cold, tight and sad. I cry, I ache. Most days I long for eyes to see me, but I stay hidden. I have to hide where none can see. For, if they see me they will despise me. 'Help' I say inside my prison. I scream, but upon my face I smile. If you were to look more closely at my eyes you might see the pain. Maybe it's just too uncomfortable for you. You see, if you notice my pain, you might feel obliged to do something about it. This would take effort and mean you might become unpopular yourself... I wouldn't want to disturb your equilibrium.

I've been brave; I've tried. But, from openness comes pain. There are those who want to close my door, who trample my little girl. So light and gay is she, but oh so sensitive. Too many times others have driven her in. 'Come out little girl' I coax. But, she just sits and mopes. No longer can I coax her out. 'Are you sleeping little girl?' Lord send some-one to love her to life once more.

What is Time?

I tried to climb the big oak tree
Scampered across and scraped my knee.
I walked for hours, picked some flowers.
If only I could just be me!

I watched the boy who lived next door.
He had a kite, I watched it soar
He had a bike, the boy next door
He had a car, I heard it roar.

The boy next door then moved away,
So did his kite and bike and car, they say.
I watched and listened, just in case,
But they were gone and in their place
The boy next door just was no more.

So did they really exist, or were they just a dream?
How can they be there and then be not?
Is it like something that Wendy forgot?

Lost

The movement is all around me,
Their lips, their hands, their faces.
The words come tumbling like a mighty sea,
With waves and without spaces.

The movement then slides away,
I know it will come another day.
When it does I'll know what to say.
But, it'll be too late,
They'll have moved away.

I feel this rush inside of me.
I move, I want to set it free.
I open my mouth,
The movement is gone.
I know I had some wonderful song.

I wander around as my head spins with sound,
I just need more time inside this square mound.
I'll come through that doorway,
I'll know what to say.
I just need more time – maybe today?

Words

Communication, orchestration and any other 'ation'
Can lure and connive its path
On people's thoughts and other's behalf.
But what of us autistics?

We think and we ponder,
While you lot sit and wonder.
'What is exactly going on?'
You say within your mind.

We know without a doubt.
But you need time to work it out.
For us it's all so simple!
Words are what they seem to be.
To us there is no problem!

Herein lies the hitch you see,
Words for you or words for me?
We tend to view things differently!

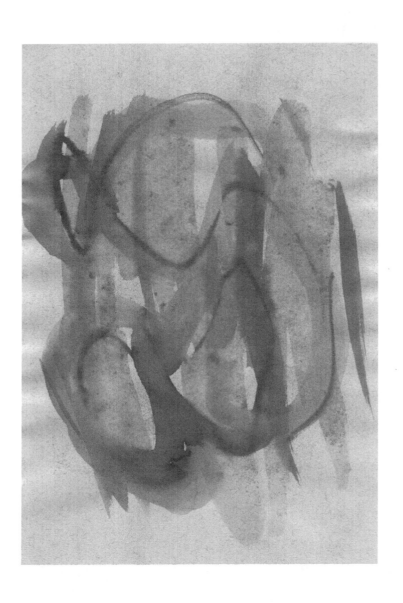

For many of us words are particularly difficult. They race towards us at great speed and then appear to collapse in a heap at the end of a sentence. By the time we have unscrambled them more sentences are piling up and they don't form nice orderly queues and wait in line to be sorted!

What do we Mean?

'You'd think the buses would run on time'
The lady says out loud.
'You mark my words, it will be fine,'
The man yells from the crowd.
I stare at each, in disbelief,
What is it that they mean?

The words we use to speak each day,
Should say the things we need to say.
But when in doubt I'll leave it out
And choose instead another way.

Space and Time

Rooms, rooms and more rooms, all filled with spaces and faces.
Some stand up and some sit down, others lie or just move
  around.
No one is right and no one is wrong.
Words that are spoken are heard and then gone.
Time is important and then it is not, it was for a moment and
  then I forgot.
So, I write all this down and I just hang around,
Looking and watching and listening to sound.
Please be clear, and say it like it is,
Then I might hear you, and understand what 'this' means.

Travellers

Life is a journey for travellers: we are all just passing through.
However, life can be so different, for either me or you.
A word spoken in anger can wound eternally,
A word spoken in kindness can set the hurting free.

'I have set before you life or death'
Which is it that you choose?
The roads can lead you either way,
But with one road we lose.

To choose to live, take tomorrow's hand,
To choose to give, take Love's fair stand.
If you desire a life that's free,
Then pay the price and follow me.

The way can be long and weary,
When travelling alone,
But the journey's sweet, when friends we meet,
Who help us find our home.

Change

Change, change and more change,
Of context, place and time.
Why is it that Life's transient stage
Plays such havoc with my mind?

You said 'We'll go to McDonald's'
But this was just a thought.
I was set for hours,
But the plan then came to naught.

My tears and confused frustration,
At plans that do not appear,
Are painful beyond recognition
And push me deeper into fear.

How can life be so determined?
How can change be so complete?
With continuity there is no end.
Security and trust are sweet.

So, who said that change would not hurt me?
Who said my 'being' could not be safe?
Change said 'You need continuity,
In order to find your place.'

For change makes all things different.
They no longer are the same.
What was it that you really meant?
All I feel is the pain.

I often moved house as a child and lived in various counties in England, UK. Although I wasn't good at playing with other children and it appeared that I hardly noticed other people, I did become attached to things. Even today I can tell you the colour of the bedroom I shared, as a nine-year-old with my sisters. I can describe the pattern on the curtains, the lino in the bathroom and the grey windbreak outside our back door. But, apart from a favoured bicycle that became mangled when it and I collided with a bus, I can't think of any special 'toy' or child that I considered my 'bestest'! I do remember the radio, whose music often calmed me.

Moving Away

Home is where the heart is,
Or so some people say.
Home is what I'm leaving,
On this fine summer's day.

So fare thee well, Oh dwelling place,
'Tis time for moving on.
I bid you adieu, and turn my face,
For I must needs be gone.
My journey leads me thither,
To another home I must go.
Its vision calls me hither,
To explore and then to know.
'Tis home with all the others,
A place for time to share,
It calls, just like our mothers,
As they swoop us up with care.

This music calms my fears
And brings dancing to my heart.
But to my eyes still come the tears,
As you and I must part.

Routine

I feel your presence inside of me,
I hear your voice when you ask to see.
But which is which and what is what?
I did remember, and then forgot.

I think I need this very thing,
But how can I know for sure?
Is it really what I need?
Should I ask for more?

More information, more advice?
Do I need a bigger slice?
Do I need it?
Do I want it?
Is it really worth the price?

Most of the time I cannot tell.
How do others know so well?
I think I'll pass on this small choice,
I think I'll find a bigger voice.

A voice of definites; absolutes and all.
A voice that is never small or tall.
A voice that says there's much and more.
A voice that I can trust for sure,
Routine.

Discovering Self

Discovering who we are and understanding ourselves can take us all a long time. Usually, though, when asked, most people can tell you their favourite music, colour, supermarket, book, TV programme and so on. I was quite good with factual information concerning things of my interest, but getting a handle on 'me' has taken me much longer than most. Perhaps one of my biggest shocks was self-discovery. Insight can be a positive thing, but if all it does is illuminate one's difficulties, then it might not be seen as a bonus.

So This is Me!

Tweedle dee and tweedle dum,
How on earth have I begun?
I started out all right you see,
But now I question 'who is me?'

Which of these I know so well,
How I wish that I could tell.
If only it could stay the same,
I'd work the rules out for this game.

They call the movie 'Life' you see,
But which is them and which is me?
I know for me the words serve well,
But as for others, who can tell?
I thought I'd got it,
But then came the shock.
You lot knew it,
But I did not!

Questions

The world rushes by,
It doesn't notice us.
We see with our eyes
All the horrible stuff.
In being here and standing still,
Notice we surely will,
But, the world rushes by,
Leaving always the question 'why?'

Wendy

Fair-skinned and freckled, podgy, pedantic and particular;
    that's me.
Dark hair, not so tall, I need glasses to help me see.
I rescue beetles, ants and spiders,
I love water, shades and 'Sliders'.*
Science fiction, books about nature, birds, butterflies and bush.
Pussy cats, dogs, sunshine and rainbows,
These are the things that turn me to mush.

I don't like mathematics; numbers make me hurt.
Can't trust me with money or leave me with the purse.
I'll work it all out, sort of.
Get there in the end.
But in the meanwhile there is this trend,
Wendy loses another friend.

I'm good at the things I do so well.
But, 'Oh dear' with the things I do not.

* 'Sliders' is a milkshake.

I am a Sexual Being Too

I feel you loving me today
I hear your voice, as it drifts this way.
I'll give you breakfast on the floor,
We'll go for a walk across the moor.

Companion faithful and oh so true,
The love of my life,
It could only be you.
I see you standing across the hall.
I notice your smile against the red wall.
Maybe one day I'll be that tall?
I'd like you to stay and not go away,
But, you don't and you can't,
And you're not here today.

I have all of these feelings that tumble around.
I'm not sure I like them,
Certainly don't want them,
How can I make them go back underground?

They won't go away, I hear your voice say.
You have to sort them, they're here to stay.
But I don't understand them, their voice is too loud.
They make me do things,
Especially in a crowd.

'No, Wendy, not here' your louder voice states.
'That should be in private, and not for this place'
What is for private and what is this place?
I wish I could read the look on your face.

I Used To... But Now I...

I used to be much smaller but now I am much taller.

I used to ride my walker but now I am a talker.

Skipping rope was what I liked but that was before I got my
bike.

My dog Rusty loved to swim, without warning she'd jump
right in!

My sisters used to tease me bad, so when I could I teased them
back.

I used to think to smoke was cool, but now I know I was a
fool.

To be a nurse would be unreal, is what I used to always feel.

Now I want to know much more and see what lies through a
different door.

So I can tell, from these few words, that as I grow and get to
know just who

Who I am and why I came, I may not need to stay the same.

Who I am and why I came, I may not need to stay the same.

My Body

Heads and shoulders, knees and toes, knees and toes,
This is how the saying goes.
But what of pubic hair that grows?
Of penis, vagina, breasts and those?

What of feelings, periods and figures?
Why do we have them?
Is it the same for Jane, Tom and Ben?
Can we identify all of the triggers?

Do I have to go through this?
Could I not just give it a miss?
I was OK before all of these changes,
Now I erupt into multiple rages.

Now I have feelings I didn't feel before.
Now I have times I can't go out the door.
Now I want what I had before,
But also my body desires so much more.

My mind cannot keep up with all of these things,
My head takes me places where my heart rarely sings.
But then what to do and what should I say?
I think it is best if it just all goes away!

Care

Tall, handsome, with large brown eyes.
Someone that you know?
Do you hear him as he cries
Or is it that you have to go?
There's a baby in the park,
They say she'll be a beauty.
But she's left alone, in the dark
After all – it's not our duty.

He's very good at football
And I'm sure he'll make the team.
Shame about his mother's fall
They say she was a scream.

Indecision 2

To decide – can't decide.
Just get well, when up you come.
You raise your ugly head in defiance
'No, no, no,' you cry, 'I'm not dead – I'm here and I always will
    be, you can't get away from me.'

Which one and when?
Is it now I'm supposed to love?
Or was it yesterday?

I can't love you here – only hate – aggression.
The moments of time aren't on my side. So little time, and
Death lies around the corner.
You follow me, seeking, always seeking like shadows, empty
    shadows.
Trying to impress the others, or me?
What should I wear? Who am I today?
Which one is me?

You both struggle and fight inside of me
You both want your freedom
Sometimes I want to be you,
Most of the time I am striving to stay me – confusion.
How to decide. Can't decide.

Autism Is

Autism is: being present in this world,
But not entirely of it.
I am one step removed and curled,
The switch just doesn't click.
I perform the role of my perception,
And play many parts so well.
But minus files for my redemption,
My part in life I cannot tell.

Life is like a video,
I watch but cannot partake.
My uneven skills are but an echo
Of the frustrations which I hate!

However, my focused use of time and space
I would not give away.
I know that I am especially placed
For some developed career one day!

So This is Life

Stagnant cool unprotected.
An endless ocean of non-entity.
Shapeless visions greying in a colourless void.
Light dominates the passivity of my reflection.
Feeling, many feelings, linking up but not with each other.

Aggression, hate, love, indifference.
Which one and when?
Is it now I'm supposed to respond, or was it yesterday?
'Would you like a bag, Wendy?' What is 'like'? How can I
    know?
The moments of time aren't on my side. So little time, and
Decisions need to be made. All the silence tells me is
    'Nothing'.
You follow me, seeking, always seeking. You are like shadows,
    empty shadows.
What should I wear? Who am I today?
Which one should I be? How to decide. Can't decide.
Chaos, confusion – too many choices!
Feeling lost.

Retreat, soft, gentle, warm. Every thing still.
Green, fading into distant mist. Divided into hills, trees,
    nothing.
Touching the blue-grey, sky. Unbroken; heat, muzzy, stormy.
Breeze, soft, gentle, warm. Every thing still.
All the people have gone.
The decisions have left.

Walking

Walking, not talking,
Along this sunlit path.
The trees rise beside me,
The wind rushes past.
I hear the birdsongs echo,
The rustle of the leaves,
I feel so contented,
Caught in this moment's breeze.
How wondrous is the springtime,
With new life all around.
The death of wintry coldness,
Has since gone underground.

I know we need the wintertime,
I know death has to come.
But for this springtime moment,
My heart and soul are one.

Relationships

I didn't choose my parents and they did not choose me.
We are quite different people, it's certainly plain to see.
Although we share some common features,
Passed on from them to me,
We are all individuals and different we will be.

Now difference poses problems that arise for one and all.
Some of us are short and some of us are tall.
Some of us like quietness, solitude and all,
Whilst others like it noisy, chaotic and much more.

Relating to others will mean finding common ground.
I need to notice that there's more than me around.
For this to happen with success it takes us both you see,
I need to notice you and you to notice me.

There are degrees of friendship, this is how it should be.
Some people are polite to all but choose more sensibly
Those to spend their time with, those they should ignore,
Those they can work with and those that they adore.

Unfortunately there is no 'one size that fits all',
In fact, some will tell you 'all is fair in love and war'.
So if the rules keep changing and people will change too,
How can you relate to me and I relate to you?

We are Walking Through the Valley

We are walking through the valley,
The larks sing on the wing.
My head thinks thoughts so merry,
My heart just longs to sing.

Grass of green and sky of blue,
You will be my witness.
With all of these a sweet bucket,
I know my heart can rest.

But then the pathway leads me on,
Over stream, gorge and glen.
The mountain ranges rise ahead,
As darkness fills the days instead.

My feet and heart no longer know
The way to find the valley.
The restful place I walked before
Now lies beyond the forest door.

How did I end up in this place?
Why do the larks not sing?
What's happened to my valley safe?
I'm lost inside this 'nothing'.

I need to find my way back home,
But home seems to have gone.

Adulthood

We all grow up and get older. Earning one's moccasins takes time and effort. Earning self-respect can be difficult if we measure ourselves against the standards set by others. I am learning that being human means failure, and failure, although painful, is part of the process that leads to success. I have gotten so many things wrong; relationships, employment, decisions, choices and so on. However, now, as a grown-up, I can choose whether or not I allow those to dictate to me and my future, or whether I weave them into the tapestry of my life and allow them to add texture and tone to my life. I choose the latter.

ASD: My Gender

My gender and I are a package.
We come as part of the deal.
'But autism shows far more damage.'
'Look at the things that you feel.'

I cannot account for these feelings.
Emotions intense and extreme.
But my issues with everyday dealings
Can cause me to rant, shout and scream.

I don't desire the make-up.
Fashion and high-heels don't appeal.
I don't like perfume or my hair cut,
But my need for 'understanding' is real.

The expectations placed upon me,
Being female and all,
Push me further into pain and grief,
With my back against the wall.

'I cannot multi-task,' I say.
'But you must, you're a woman. You can.'

You must cook, clean, organize and play
The role that supports your man.

Your children and men depend on you,
You must be strong, in control and sure.
'What if these things I cannot do?'
'What if my timing is poor?'

'You must work harder, try harder to be
What society says and dictates.'
'But both my autism and gender are me, you see
They both influence my states.'

As a woman I function differently.
As a woman I think, see and feel.
As a woman I value *all* that is me.
My autism is part of the deal.

I married at the age of 20 and had my first child at 22. The poem below was written for him. Some say that individuals with autism can't relate to others and, therefore, parenting will be difficult for them. I think being a parent is difficult for anyone, and for most of us loving our children is a choice; not just a feeling.

Miracle

Baby, baby, sleeping sound, where is it that you go?
To the forest, underground, to the sea, or snow?
You seem to lie so still and quiet;
Can I share your dreams?
I will love and care for you, whatever that may mean.
When you feel sad or very glad, I want to hear your voice.
Communication may be tough, but it will be our choice.

So often we each find ourselves as part of a group or gathering. What if one didn't understand the unwritten rules of mutual communication? What if one's interests dictated one's attention and crowded out the concept of shared interests?

The Group

There were just seven of us,
Seated all around.
The man with the shortest hair
Started to make a sound.
I was quiet.
I wanted to keep watching,
There were blue tits in the tree.
The man said something louder,
'Oh, did you speak to me?'
I said.

'There are blue tits in the tree,'
Said I. There was silence in the group.
The man with the shortest hair
Returned to eating his soup.

'There are blue tits in the tree,'
I stated just once more.
'Wendy, do you want some tea?'
'Do you want me to pour?'
He said.

'There are blue tits in the tree,'
I only thought this time.
'Why were they not excited?'
'Could they not enjoy this find?'
They all ate soup.

'Wendy, the waiter needs to clear the plates,'
The man with the shortest hair spoke.
'Why does this concern me?' I said.
The girl with long hair spoke,
'You need to eat your soup now, Wendy,
Hurry up for goodness' sakes!'

What had I done?
What did I not get?
The blue tits are gone,
I haven't eaten yet.

What is Love?

I have tulips on the table, bright red buds of life.
When I look at them my smile grows,
I ponder the springtime and all that it shows;
The new life of ducklings, saplings and bulbs.
This must be love.

I have dinner dished in front of me,
A tasty meal to nourish.
This food enriches my body,
My soul will also flourish.
This must be love.
I encounter some pleasant talking,
I enjoy the woods a-walking,
I feel the sun's face and touch some tender place.
My hurts are all healed as I upward yield.
This must be love.

But what of harsh words and looks that could kill?
Can love reign here too, or is it just still?
Maybe it moves over as pain moves back in,
Maybe it dies when it knows it can't win?
This must be love.

Commitment

To you this day my words I say that offer you my pledge.
The days ahead before us spread, bring us to the edge.
Now life can sing and to us bring the joy of love that's shed,
To bring us peace and sweet release,
As in our heart our fears depart,
Our stage, contentment, helps us start.

The road that winds or twists and twines,
Our future will unfold.
Together we walk and talk,
Together get to know and grow.
For in our sharing of ups and downs,
Our journey leads us on.
You with me and me with you,
We'll understand and be at one.

With grace her wings now spread
To you my love,
This day my dove,
I offer you my pledge.

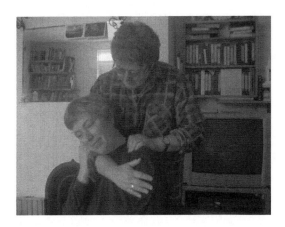

My daughter Katy had a tumultuous time moving from England to Australia; well, all of us did really. However, although she battled chronic fatigue as a young teenager and struggled to complete Years 11 and 12, she made it! Then, her first marriage ended after two years and Katy just wanted to drive her car into a tree. Instead, she plucked up the courage to hang on in there and explore other potential horizons. The poem below was written for her on the day of her marriage to Stu, an English lad from Staffordshire. Today, seven years after they first met they are building a home and life together in Australia. That's my Katy, little lady, and I love her!

Katy's Getting Married

Katy is my daughter and I've known her all her life.
Today is the day that she becomes Stu's wife.
Although she was born wide-eyed and cheeky-grinned,
She's always had a generous heart that welcomed us all in.

When she was just a toddler, with less hair than even I,
She liked to kid around a lot, a finger in every pie.
Mischievous as a kitten and so direct you'd die,
She'd tell you what she thought of things, including you and I.

As Katy began to grow, her hair a strawberry blonde,
The sunlight kissed and played with her,
The rain, the wind formed bond
In fact, even on the greyest days her smile had us all conned.

When standing in her presence, however you did feel,
She had this way of cheering you, my cheeky little girl.
Then, along came Australia and childish whims gave flight.
The sunny days of England turned from daytime into night.

The home of fields, woods and raspberry cane
Where all had been delight,
Became an urban jungle, familiarity gave flight,
And nothing was the same.

Family ties were challenged,
The cornflakes didn't taste right.
The people spoke with funny accents
Poisonous spiders, snakes and Vegemite.

The years rolled on and joy rolled out
So many things did change,
Katy's health, home and friends,
An era for many different trends.

Some were welcome, some were not,
Some were times now best forgot.
The good news is that through it all
My Katy came out trumps.
No more measles, chicken pox,
No chronic fatigue or mumps.

No more confusion, Katy knows she's backed a winner.
All the doubt now in the past,
Today's the day, it's here at last.
The future now looks settled.

With Stu beside her, shackles cast
The home front now in view,
Katy darling all is well,
The Lord is blessing you.

So, to this happy couple,
On this, their chosen day,
Our Katy and our Stuart,
We are with you all the way.

Words 2

Every thought I ever had was made of someone's words.
Every picture I can see consists of words so perfectly.
In this understanding though,
There is such a lot to know.
What if I get it wrong?

I thought I had the picture right,
I thought I had the words that night.
Then the person looked my way,
'What was it that you tried to say?'
They didn't know.

Why were they not listening?
Why didn't they understand?
To me it makes such utter sense,
Yet they just 'beat around the fence'.
I don't get it!

I use words to say exactly what I mean.
I use words to say only what is seen.
I use words to show where I have been.
I use words because they are a beam.
What do they show?

They tell us that we all think things,
They show and tell their act.
The difficulty here with words is obviously a fact.
You have your words and I have mine,
They may not be the same.
Please teach me what your words might mean,
And I will teach you mine.

Although our words describe for us the path our life road
    takes,
They may lead to different maps,
They may produce big wide gaps.
What does your map show?

I want our words to cross over.
I want mine to meet with yours.
I want to come out from 'under cover'.
Can I trust you with my course?
Will you listen?

Thank you for saying you will.
Thank you for being here still.
You in your world and I in mine,
Together sharing some space.
Together we're building, this time.

Seasons

Sandy shadows of yesterday
Swaying to and fro from mind,
Relive the patterns of today.
Though sometimes drift behind.

I remember and then forget
My summer days linger on
The shades as night are always set
Like a memory, then it's gone.

The leaves are rustling crisp
As autumn blows its way.
The winter you can't miss
But spring will have her say.

Seasons of night pass on into eternity
Sandwiched between dream and reality
Is the world of fantasy.
Have you been there?

A land of midnight, music and fair.
Drifting between love and freedom,
The wind blowing through your hair.
The white moon casts shadows
Silver, grey and shades of pale.

The old woman sits and sews
And the young girl eagerly reads her mail.
Hoping for love, hoping for laughter
It never rains but it pours,
Sometimes, never and always as after.

Absences... Left or right
Pain –
Chaos, confusion – too many choices!
Feeling lost.

My Love

It wasn't always this way. The joy of knowing you
And sharing in your life has taught me that I am
Able to love and accept myself. In your presence
I come to life in a way that I have never experienced before. This
     rag doll who is losing her stuffing becomes the musical clown,
So full of colour and vitality.
You set me free from the demands of self introspection and its
     ugly forest of gloom.
In its place I am able to walk through sunlit woods
And enjoy choruses of bird song.

Your smile delights my eyes and the peace in my soul
Rolls over me like the gentle waves of a calm ocean.
So soothing is your voice to my ears that even the roar
Of my lions within cannot shatter it.
Thank you, my love, for your quiet assurance and humble
     vulnerability.
To you I owe a never-ending debt, my life.

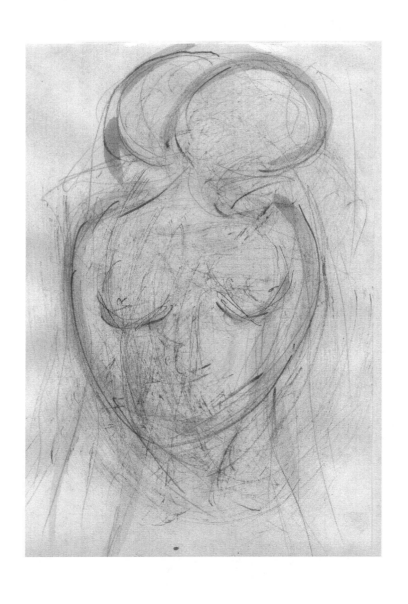

Time For

The seconds seem to tick away,
As there goes the end of another day.
Did I do all I wanted to?
Did I say what I needed to?

Will I get time to revisit this day?
Can I regain what I lost on the way?
Will time keep my secrets safe and sound,
Or will I discover that they have been found?

I waste so much time in my fear of 'the time',
I lose so much joy with stress in my mind.
Oh to relax and appreciate 'Time'.
Oh to know 'Safe', please throw me a line.

I've given you 'Time', Wendy.
'Tis there for your needs.
I want you to recognize all of its seeds.
Using them wisely allows 'time' to grow.
Take 'time' to wander.
Take 'time' to know.

I'm clumsy, hyperactive and find it hard to tell
That the time has come to stop.
'I must sort this now. I can't go to sleep'.
'Oh yes you must. Now, not another peep.'

I toss and I turn all through the long night.
I want sleep to come but it's far out of sight.
So, up I get once more to turn my computer on.
If I cannot sleep in bed I'll not stay,
But I can write through out this next day.

I Know

You touched my life, you entered me.
Life will never be quite the same again.
I still hurt inside, I try to hide, I still want you here, at my side.

Letting go of you and ending pursuit,
Is very hard to say.
I look for your affirmation, telling me I am OK.

Knowing love just isn't enough,
Knowing the past is still full of stuff.
Knowing I'll make it, in spite of this pain.
Knowing I'll be OK once again.

Going through separation and divorce is very strange and very different from being married and together. For me being married took a great deal of adjusting to. In some ways, it took less time to adjust to being on my own. Today I am thankful to my long time partner for her patience and commitment to me and to my children. Christmas, Easter and birthdays were important when the children were growing up. They still are, but there are more memories from when the children were younger. Staying 'in touch' with their lives now as adults is harder. They have their own friends, work places and interests. This is how it should be, but at times I miss being more involved with them. I guess I just want for them to be OK.

Easter 1992

Tim

Although this room is purple, green is the way to go.
Take one step forward, then turn left, now take five steps
    in a row.
From where you stand, eyes toward the ground,

Open the lid and you have found
Your edible chocolate rabbit.

Matt

This cream-walled room will hold your dream
But from the doorway this can't be seen.
Take five steps forward and then turn left.
Five more steps forward and you can rest.

Beneath the mountain lies your chest.
One delicious chocolate rabbit.

The next four poems were written when I was a teenager. I remember being taken up with the discovery of the air when it moved (the breeze) or with the quietness of no one.

Mr Breeze

Lovingly he bends the reeds
That nod the heads of daffodils.
To make his point he shakes the trees
Or creeps across our window sills.

The Quiet

Soft, gentle, warm
Every thing still.
Green, fading into distant mist,
Divided into hills, trees, nothing
Touching the blue, grey, sky
Unbroken; heat, muzzy, stormy
Breeze, soft, gentle warm
Every thing still.
All the people have gone.
No birds, no dogs, no children.
Just myself and me.

Sometimes

Sometimes my thoughts are all in rhymes,
Sometimes they are not,
Words are words which say a
Lot, sometimes;
Sometimes they do not.
I am running out of things
To write
So maybe I should stop
The day is turning into night
And this really is my lot.

Doubt

Seasons of night pass on into eternity
Sandwiched between dream and reality
Is the world of fantasy.
Have you been there?
A land of mid-night, music and fair.
Drifting between love and freedom,
The wind blowing through your hair.

The white moon casts shadows
Silver, grey and shades of pale.
The old woman sits and sews
And the young girl eagerly reads her mail
Hoping for love, hoping for laughter
It never rains but it pours
Sometimes never and always as after.

Love

You light up my life, yes,
Like a candle at nighttime,
Like a lamp in the storm
Like a fire in the cold.
With the glow of your warm smile
And the sunshine of your love
You spread light and hope into this hurt heart of mine.
May the symbol of your joy
Now echoed in these colours
Always surround you, yes,
Wrap you in warmth and bathe you in life,
From this day forward, for the rest of your life.

Seasons 2

Sandy shadow of yesterday
Swaying to and fro from mind,
Relive the patterns of today.
Though sometimes drift behind.
I remember and then forget
My summer days linger on
The shades as might, are always set
Like a memory, then it's gone.
The leaves are rustling crisp
As autumn blows its way.
The winter you can't miss
But spring will have her say.

I was staying with a family in the wintry month of December, 1993. I cele-brated part of the Christmas season with them. It was all quite strange and different. I wanted to hide and I was fearful of all that I didn't understand.

The Season of Advent in a Small Swiss Village

Still the night, holy the night,
All is calm, all is tonight...
The cold damp air rushes past me. The church bells are getting
    louder now, more insistent, threatening 'Hurry up, hurry
    up.'
The hour strikes six o'clock and I just make it through the door
    as the last dong of the big bell sounds out.
Inside, all is quiet and very dimly lit. Amongst 70 or so people
    about eight candles give out the only light.

The priest begins with his chant in Latin and the heads in front
    of me respond with equal anonymity.

There is no sound here. The sweat runs down my back as a
    response is squeezed out of my body. The cold to the warm
    breeds discomfort – no matter, I will soon adjust.

I linger, not understanding the foreign words whispered
    around me, but trying to 'get into the spirit' of things.

Alas, I fail! However, the service comes to a close and the
    masses file out into the community hall for breakfast.
Down here the candles glow brighter and the nameless faces
    form smiles.

The lights bounce and shimmer in the children's eyes and the
grown-ups stir the silence with loud laughter.

Much conversation transpires and the older folk of the village
talk of 'long ago', and 'when I was a child...'

Coffee is passed around as the white bread is buttered and
spoonfuls of jam are dolloped onto small plates. In between
the various stories, small children giggle and teenagers
blush – the men share achievements and stories as the
winter rains continue down the battened glass panes of the
church hall.

Inside my heart a door opens. Somewhere in the days of
yesteryear a memory is brought forth for today. It is good
to be here. For a few moments, maybe even a season, my
own dragon is lost in the community of hard knocks; the
softness of this time is soothing. For how long will this
gentle reality cover my pain...?

The dreams of abandonment still wait in the wings and I know
that they will return to haunt me.
My task at this time is to soak in as much of this Holy Season
as my heart will allow. As the warmth of its cards and
candles lap at the corners of my soul, I will take hope as
my anchor. Together we will have the strength to undo
those darkest deeds and disarm the dastardly dragon that
seeks to rob and destroy the musical chimes.

The innocence of childhood can be unmasked with safety, but
only at a distance and within the context of Christmas.

So come, Christ child, come into these unexpressed memories
and corners of the mind and push out the darkness with its
clammy clinging fingers – Be gone – you are not wanted
here – life has better things to offer!

Indecision

To decide – can't decide.
Just get well, when up you come.
You raise your ugly head in defiance
'No, no, no' you cry, 'I'm not dead – I'm here and I always will
    be, you can't get away from me.'

This next poem was written between the ages of 17 and 20, during the early years of my internment in a mental institution in England. I was being 'treated' for mental illness and was given quite large amounts of anti-psyhotic medication. It might seem like the thing to do, medication I mean, but it may only dull our senses and leave us more alone than ever.

Where is Wendy?

Stagnant cool unprotected.
An endless ocean of non-entity.
Shapeless visions graying in a colorless void.
Light dominating the passivity of my reflection
Feeling, many feelings, linking up but not with each other
Aggression, hate, love, indifference.
Which one and when?
Is it now I'm supposed to love?
Or was it yesterday?

I can't love you here – only hate – aggression.
The moments of time aren't on my side. So little time, and
Death lies around the corner.
You follow me, seeking, always seeking like shadows, empty
    shadows.
Trying to impress the others, or me?
What should I wear? Who am I today?
Which one is me?

You both struggle and fight inside of me
You both want your freedom
Sometimes I want to be you,
Most of the time I am striving to stay me – confusion.

How to decide. Can't decide.

Today

Jungle, deeply cut into the interior,
Dark dense speckled with the inevitable light of the season's
    sun.
I wish that you were here, we have so much to share,
So little in common.

The rain falling steadily at day break,
Meaning to wake the sleepy spiders and remind the blackbird of
Its long lost song.

Puddles, murky and solemn, like cold porridge on a winter's day.
Sometimes it's hard to remember when you're feeling far away,
Just what it was like when children used to play.

Empty Thoughts

I want to write something creative, but my mind is empty and
I cannot think. Like after the sun has gone down and
The birds have stopped singing. Maybe you're supposed to live
    in the realm of reason; or is it logic?
Does despair have its roots in the key of C, or is it G?
Could it be that the black threads of night have woven their
    way into a life
Filled with fear and doubt?
I think truth is around, it just has to be found.
Like a rook who builds her nest up high, just to touch the edge
    of the sky.
Will we leave her hopes to die,
Or croak for something better?

Part of my university course entailed having a supervisor for some months of practical experience. I was fortunate; my supervisor and I were able to relate quite well. The poem below was written for her.

Ode to a Supervisor

It came to me one awesome night, when all the stars were
    shining bright.
I did say 'yes it'll be all right!' 'Tis just a pastoral student.
Someone who'll care, someone who'll share in all the daily
    tasks. No matter if they're learnin', or are not sure of the
    way, the questions they asks, the periods of dismay, 'tis all
    part and parcel of the package I will say.
They come to me with willin' hearts, so well versed in all their
    parts, 'That's great,' I say, 'you 'ave done well', now pay
    attention, let me tell. You see, life's like a rainbow; red,
    yellow, blue. The problem is the rain comes first and then
    the sun shines through.
So don't give up, don't be alarmed; we all fall down, 'twill do
    no 'arm. The road is long and the way is rough, but you are
    strong and you are tough. I travelled down that road
    before. I know how it feels to be unsure. I passed the test, I
    did me best, and just like you, I needed rest.

So on with the journey we must go, to far-off places we don't
    know. Over dale an' over 'ill, to distant lands we travel still.
    But through it all, come rain or shine, there'll be that
    moment in our time when we gaze through the mist of our
    windscreen visor and engage the smile of our supervisor!

At whatever stage of life we be, I need you and you need me,
    to find our place and know our space is where the journey
    leads. So 'old me hand and together let's stand as we view
    the foreign horizon, student and supervisor!

There are times when wanting and having are at loggerheads with one another. Wanting a friend and trying not to upset them — a game played where one must find the balance between give and take, between demand and independence. I was never much good at finding the centre of the universe and maintaining it!

Torment

I couldn't welcome sleep tonight,
The restful peace had ceased.
Just torment tossed became my plight,
As quilt about me creased.

The words of a hymn raged within,
While all without just seemed to shout,
'You're all locked in. There's no way out!'
Oh to have wings and upwards spout!

But there must be a better way, beyond this turmoil insane.
The battered ocean's sandy shore will turn calm again.
Do I have the strength to stand and call the winds to blow?
Will tomorrow bring relief, or will it onward go?

I can't remain in this dark storm with edges jagged as,
I want the game of 'tug' to stop and all the pain to pass.
If I allow the rope to drop and exit off the stage,
Will the clouds cease to roll, the storm cease to rage?

I want to share 'myself' with you and let you see the
     frightened 'me'.
But if I do will you still play? Or will it mean the end of day?
If I am here, to be and stay, I need acceptance all the way.
I don't just mean acknowledgement, a waving hand, or place to
     stand.

I need true acceptance, my autism comes as well.
I can't be neurotypical, and read the signs that tell,
What's happening for you or them, for Jane or Jim or
      John or Ben.
I need true acceptance; my autism does as well.

What is My Name?

You call my name. 'Come play a game.'
'We want you here with us.'
I hear you not, in Time's forgot,
'Leave Wendy out. She's lost the plot.'
You laugh at me, you run away,
I'm so glad you didn't stay.
But angry or discomfort now,
Could mean for me the biggest row!

'I want to be like Superman'
The answer to all things is "He can",
His name gives hope,
He don't smoke dope.
He doesn't sit around and mope!

'Why can't I be like him?'
'Why do I not fit in?'
'I'm not the same, can't play your game,
What, I wonder, is in my name?'

You called my name, your tone was soft.
I looked at you with questioning eyes…
'It's OK' you said, 'I will not scoff.'
You noticed my fear and my surprise.

'Am I really welcome here?'
'You'll soon get fed up with me.'
'Well, if I do I'll just tell you so,
We'll work it out, so have no fear.'

'But I so often get it wrong.'
'We all do that my friend.'
But what if I hurt you?'
You will, I'll mend.'

So, how can I know if I should go,
When to be fast, or to be slow?
When to speak or silence show,
It's your turn now; you have a go.

We'll learn together, explore this land.
But you must allow me to hold your hand.
It won't be easy, but we'll stand our ground,
And come out triumphant, our friendship sound.

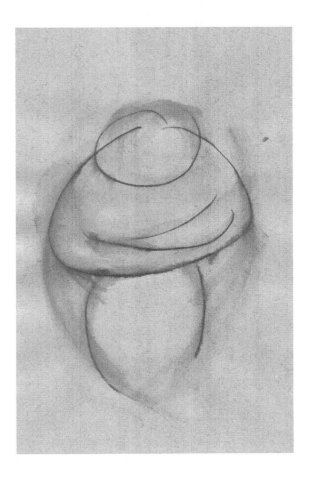

Autism Is (Also)

The world for me,
Where I can be.
Where I can see.
Where I am free.

Autism is who I am,
What I can.
Why I ran.
Because I can.

Your world is different.
You don't run.
You know what is meant.
Life can be such fun.

You hide your fear well,
So no one can see.
I haven't learnt this,
I can only be me.

Joan and Bob

Joan and Bob
Bound together
For always and ever,
Like Scottish heather.

Bob's gone on ahead,
It was his time.
It isn't yours
And it isn't mine.

But his humour
He leaves us.
His 'och' and his 'ay'.
They never leave us
For memories can't die.

They live in our hearts,
The words that he spoke.
For he really was
Such a likeable bloke.

Death is only the winter at noon.
All comes to life again.
The spring will come soon
Though winter is cold,
And lonely for some,
We've his love in our hearts,
This will keep our souls warm.

Friendship

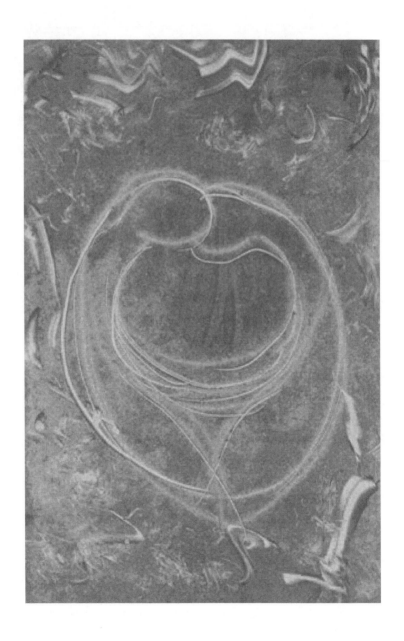

For Emma

When you are far across the sea
Over there and not near me,
Remember that where'er you be
'Tis with the heart that truth we see.

And when you really want to know,
If all is well…and should you go?
Then if in doubt, just leave it out,
For you can trust when to say 'no'.

Journeys lead us, we know not where,
But 'tis for sure they take us 'there'.
Sometimes for good, sometimes not,
But either way is not forgot.

So, dear beloved take all care,
Have lots of fun, know when to run.
My arms go with you,
As does my heart
For they are yours, when near or apart.

I love you.

*When my children were in secondary school we had a Japanese student
come stay with us for two years. When Ayumi left to return to Japan I wrote
her the song below. As far as I know Ayumi is now a lawyer in Tokyo.*

Ayumi's Parting Song
(*sung to the tune of 'Robin Hood'*)

Ayumi, Ayumi riding in the taxi,
Ayumi, Ayumi late for school again.
Sleeps in the day, works in the night,
Ayumi, Ayumi fights for what's right!

Ayumi, Ayumi walking the Prince's Highway.
Ayumi, Ayumi through the wind and rain,
Sleeps in the day, works in the night,
Ayumi, Ayumi fights for what's right!

Ayumi, Ayumi eating up her seaweed,
Ayumi, Ayumi drinking coffee too.
Sleeps through the day, works through the night.
Ayumi, Ayumi fights for what's right!

Ayumi, Ayumi flying through the air,
Ayumi, Ayumi will soon be over there,
Sleeping through the day, working through the night,
Ayumi, Ayumi fighting for what's right!

Feeling Safe

I wander out across the meadow allowing the wind to prance
with my hair.
Even if I had worn a hat, the chances of keeping tidy hair
would have been minimal. I can feel the lightness of the
sun's warmth on my cheek. Above me larks are singing as
they are whisked up high on currents of warm air. What a
day this is; a day of feeling. The intensity of emotion over-
whelms me. I love being here.

Here I am safe; here I am wanted. Here I am understood.
Although I cannot command my feet to dance, for my
clumsiness forbids them, my heart takes heed instead. My
dancing seems eternal and music floats out to meet me.
Even grief could not taunt the wind to carry me to a
different place. There is no place for grief here. Even in the
shadow the sun's brightness explodes any thought of
misery or pain. I hope this dance lasts a lifetime of summer
breezes and winter nights. I don't want it to end.

Happy Birthday

This comes with special wishes
For a very happy day.
For today is someone's birthday,
So it's joy in every way.
The rains they may keep coming and the winds they do blow
    strong,
But 'tis hoped your heart be gladdened by the tiny sparrow's
    song.
I'm glad God counts each hair on heads and sees the colours
    rainbows spread.
He knows our dreams and visions too.
There's nothing unseen,
In His worldview.

Each birthday as it comes and goes,
Brings laughter, sadness and it shows.
Another wrinkle doth appear,
To display the passing year.
But, these lines just help us see,
The path more clearly,
Where we be.

'Tis Wisdom, we are told,
Who gathers in the fold,
Takes care out there and invites all to share
In what she doth behold.

So, this birthday will bring a mixture of both joy and tears.
But it gives the opportunity
Of sharing someone's fears.

Whatever this day brings for you,
It's hoped with sincere wishes true,
That you will know the love,
Of those about
And Him above, and find a place
Where there is space,
To enjoy the changing taste
Of flavours old and new.

This is where my rhyme doth end,
It's come to you as any friend
Who would have you know
That in these words the heart would share
Its wish to care and joy with you.

As one can do.
That is to say,
On 'whoever's' day,
May so many things just go your way!

Attention Poem

Attention can mean so many things,
From palace guards to diamond rings.
What draws your attention?

Do you notice the little things,
Or do they pass you by?
Is it birds and mountain springs,
That tend to catch your eye?

Can you visit the world through a different time?
Can you see, as if through me?
What would you notice, if your life was mine?
Would you feel the things that are me?

Attention divided and shared amongst all,
Gives hints of a wider array.
Attention more focused, discrete and distinct,
Attempts to highlight my day.

Will you come with me and see what I see,
Or will you go your own way?
Join my attention. This is my plea.
Join my attention today.

Doubly Drawn

Your smile and eyes come dance with mine,
Your arms around me tight.
I love your voice, your youth, your prime,
Our laughter as we fight.

Your maleness and your softness,
Attract the woman in me,
Your long piano fingers,
That promise to set love free.

As much as I so love your form,
I miss the female charm.
At times I long for tender touch,
The womanly kiss, I miss so much.

What am I to do with all these things I feel?
They take over my life and present as so real.
But this reality may not have a place,
I'm torn in two by each different face.

This world with all its taboos and rules,
Does not allow for love that duals,
That switches off from thee to me,
From she to he and back to me!

I'm somewhere in between the two,
My love for him and love for you.
In an ideal world you both would do,
But I know my ideal cannot come true.

So, as a way of compromise,
And to avoid regret,
Longing for the both of you
I live my life, a secret.

Acceptance by others?
Could be a dream come true.
Oh to be just understood,
You'll see I'm just like you.

Wendy (Take 2)

Fair skinned and freckled, podgy, pedantic and particular,
    that's me.
Dark hair, not so tall, I need glasses to help me see.
I rescue beetles, ants and spiders,
I love water, shades and 'Sliders'.

Science fiction, books about nature, birds, butterflies and bush.
Pussy cats, dogs, sunshine and rainbows,
These are the things that turn me to mush.

I don't like mathematics; numbers make me hurt.
Can't trust me with money or leave me with the purse.
Saddened by indifference, intolerance and pain,
Happy to be autistic, glad to be on this train.

The Tree of Life

I am a seed hidden in a very dark place.
I am a seed designed to seek the sun's face.
I am a seed, to grow I need space.
I am a seed. I am a seed.

I am a sapling reaching for the rain.
I am a sapling with stems that need to train.
I am a sapling whose buds will sprout again.
I am a sapling. I am a sapling.

I am a tree with branches tall and wide.
I am a tree where birds can safely hide.
I am a tree whose seeds I will provide.
I am a tree. I am a tree.

Rain

Splat, splat the rain drops fall,
Splat, splat they land upon the cat!
Splat, splat they land upon the mat,
Splat, splat the raindrops fall.

Swish, swish the wipers move,
The rain drops off the windscreen.
Swish, swish the rain drops groove,
As they dance to keep the view clean.

Splosh, splosh the rain dives deep,
It flows over the water spout.
Splosh, splosh, as I try to sleep,
I hope my roof keeps the water out!

Splat, swish and splosh,
The rain drops just keep coming.
I think I'll stay inside with Josh
And not think about the plumbing!

My Princess of the Deep

You move so calmly through the blue
With majesty in all you do.
Your kingdom bows to let you through,
As turtles curtsey at sight of you.
My princess of the deep.

I watch you as you romp and play
With royal serenity for each day.
Your subjects let you have your say
As waves roll over and homage pay.
My princess of the deep.

The queen rides beside you with such pride,
She very rarely needs to chide.
For you will grow in grace and size,
And one day be your ocean's prize.
My princess of the deep.

Thank you for your calming sight,
Your voice can help me sleep at night.
It is because of you I write
So others may take joy in your delight,
My princess of the deep.

Time

It seemed to me that we were meant to meet,
How else could you explain it?
So many times I'd walked that street,
So many times sat on that seat.

I know the pain of being alone,
I know the times of isolation.
You came into this time, my home,
You came and broke my desolation.

What was it that drew you to my time?
What was it that you saw?
For me you just looked so fine,
Sitting there that golden fall.

I noticed you, you noticed me,
We smiled and exchanged glances.
We shared some moments of our time,
Together we took our chances.

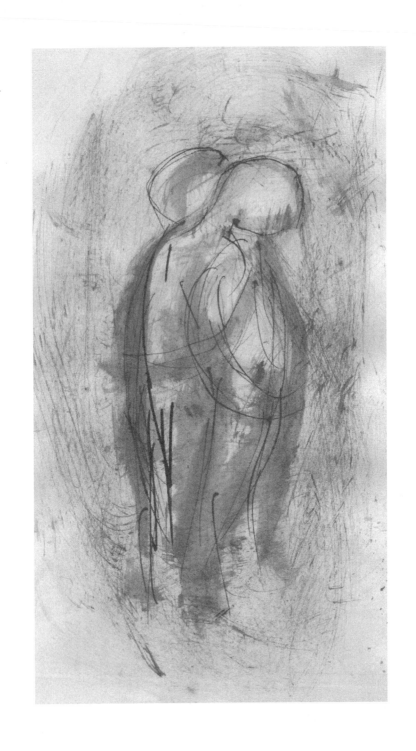

Knowing You, Knowing Me

Knowing that you know me
Makes me both glad and sad.
I want your full acceptance,
Don't want you feeling bad...

Because I am not perfect,
I'll upset you now and then.
The things that I just do not get,
Or the occasions when...

When I am most insensitive,
When I fail to see your need.
Knowing that you choose to give,
Even when I cannot read...

Read the signs you give me,
Read the needs you hold,
Knowing you forgive me,
Gives me time to be bold...

Bold in reaching out for you,
Bold in letting you reach in.
Together with our knowing,
Each new day we can begin...

Begin to grow and reach our dreams,
Begin to hold our heads up high.
Begin to reinforce those seams,
That hold the future for you and I.

The Last Supper

This wine is so symbolic
Of good friends old and true.
We hope that when you drink it
It warms you through and through.

From all of life's fair students
Who shared some time with you,
We wish you joy and prudence
In all that you will do.

May God bless your little ventures,
And the big ones too.
For all of our adventures
Come from the work we do.

So keep on being courageous,
Keep on holding the light,
So that more of life's fair students
Can travel through the night.

So now our parting paths divide,
For we are moving on.
As grapes that ripen on the vine
We sing our parting song.

To you, fine sirs, our glasses rise
We drink your health and recognize,
That you have steered us to this day.
Farewell dear friends,
We're on our way!

The Future

Life on earth is but a moment caught within the crease of time.
The seasons come and go again,
You have your life, and I have mine.

The seed that's planted within the ground
Cannot choose what to become.
A potato, an apple or a rose for some.

However, for it to be the very best,
It needs rich soil; not poor.
The sun and the rains must come,
To open that seed's door.

I may be born to nourish others,
I may delight the senses.
I may grow tall,
I may grow small,
I may stay stunted beneath wire fences.

My future may not depend on my stock,
So much as it does upon sources.
Sources of warmth, sources of care
I depend on the nurture to be for me there.

Then I can blossom and sing with the birds,
Then I can grow my potential.
So plant me in goodness and all that is fine,
Please keep the intruders away.
Give me a chance to develop, in time,
To become who I am, in life's future, one day!

Interests

Of Interest

You caught my attention today,
You happened by, just passed my way.
What was it about you that gripped me so tight?
What was it that caused me to take bait and bite?

Was it your beauty; your debonair style?
Was it your function that caused me to smile?
Was it the colour that lit up my life?
Was it not love, as man has for wife?
Whatever it was, I'm glad that you strayed,
Whatever it was, I'm happy you stayed.
Whatever it was, my attention you caught.
Whatever it was, 'twas me that you sought!

Ode to the Blackbird

The sun rises so slowly that its golden rays only just make it
    through the golden cracks in the nighttime's withdrawal.
    Even before the sun catches her breath for a broader
    attempt at the announcement of day, you are there. I can
    hear you. Your melodious song welcomes the new morn as
    a mother draws her infant towards her breast. Your singing
    calms my anxiety. Its familiarity, whatever the weather, is
    strangely warming and comforting. I count upon your
    being there. As the seasons change, so does your song, but
    still you are there. There is nothing about your form that
    strikes one as especially beautiful or endearing, but your
    song fills my heart with anticipation. Your song prepares
    the way for a day filled with bustling activity. Many
    humans will not notice you or recognize your song. Such
    busy lives, filled with wasted moments that failed to notice
    the dawn, they hurry on, and on and on. I have heard your
    song; I have noticed you. Thank you for singing.

Blue Tits

Twittering and stuttering you skip upon the wall,
With flashes of colour, blue, gold and grey.
The wintry winds puff you up as your dark cap keeps
    out the cold.
Hanging upside down you hold the skin of nuts and
    seeds so bold.
What an acrobatic fellow. Your antics always please.
I could watch you for hours whilst hiding from the breeze.

The Pelican

Just like a jumbo plane in flight
You grace our skies from dawn 'til night.
I walk around the nearby lakes
To watch you swim with swans and drakes.

With ease you catch your morning tea,
Then hoist it in the air.
It slips inside your throat, head first,
You feast without a care.

Your feathery coat so soft and downy,
Will keep the water out.
Your beady eyes that focus well,
Don't even blink when sailors shout.

You are confidence with wings,
Majestic and divine,
Though fishermen speak ill of you,
You thrill me all the time.

The Swan

Rhyme, reason, romance and rhythm, represented and rolled in
black, velvety softness. Your elegant and unassuming nature
melts the stubbornness of many a hardened human heart.
Whether dancing the tango, a gentle waltz or the two-step,
you are always 'in time' with the music. Never greedy, self-
ish or jealous, but always composed and ready. You are an
inspiration. I would like to pattern my life upon yours but,
when this isn't possible, I would like to gracefully own my
failure and swim with the ducks instead.

Flying High

As I travel between cities, towns and villages I scour the skies for your presence. Just to get a glimpse of you hovering over-head or spot you diving down to claim your prey gives me such joy. Whether you are small in frame and swift as an arrow or whether you wear stockings up to your thighs and have the most powerful talons, you are a raptor. Raptors are kings of the heavens and patrol their domains with confidence. Other birds sense your presence and bow down to you. Even those cheeky crows who will attempt to share the remains of a carcass, do so with lowered heads and tentative movement. Oh falcon, kite, eagle or hobby, alone you seem at home, but within your fam-ily circle your parenting and caring expertise know no bounds and your commitment to building the next generation should only command our respect; I am in awe of you.

Bold, Balky and Beautiful

'I couldn't imagine Christmas without it,' Jean said. I looked out across the lawn towards the lake. The pathways surrounding the water were still laden with the crisp, crunchy, golden leaves that had fallen from the deciduous trees earlier that year. Autumn really was a wondrously colourful season. 'Strange how death can be so appealing,' I thought. Then my mind returned to Jean, standing there in our kitchen in her woolly hat and mittens. Yes, winter would be here very soon and, along with it, would come Christmas. 'Well, I think turkeys deserve a better life than to be fattened up for someone's dinner, just because of tradition,' I said. 'Have you considered their feelings?' I asked. 'Whose feelings?' Jean replied. 'The turkey's feelings, of course,' I said. Jean laughed and picked up the empty casserole dish she had called over to collect. Then, as she passed by me to leave, she ruffled my hair with her fingers. 'You are funny sometimes,' she uttered, and left.

My thoughts drifted back to an earlier time when I had wondered through the bird park and had encountered the turkeys. They had made me laugh with their bright red, curly, floppy chins and funny 'gobble, gobble' sounds. Yes, I thought, lots of people every year gobble up their turkey at Christmas without a second thought about the birds themselves. I certainly had enjoyed the white meat on my Christmas dinner plate. Somehow being there and watching the birds as they walked around so freely caused me to feel guilty. I wondered why we ate this funny bird at times of thanks giving? I guess I might never understand some of the traditions that my family cherish! 'Oh well,' I thought, 'At least I don't have to perpetuate them. As a grown-up I can choose not to eat meat if I want to'.

As grown-ups we each can choose all sorts of things. It would be best if we chose wisely so that our earth could prosper and sustain its inhabitants longer. Let's not kill the whales or turkeys. Let's not imprison the bears and make them dance to tunes of pain. Let's not raid the eagle's nest and rob her of future generations. Let's not steal the ocean's fish before they have a chance to replenish their stocks. Let's not kill the forests and take away the creatures' homes. Let's not, let's not, let's not.

Song of Songs

How I love to hear your song,
Little bird so high.
You sing without the smallest throng,
Up in the bluest sky.

On days of grey,
In wind and rain,
Your song still has its say.
In spring each year, you give us cheer,
From April and through May.

'Oh for the wings of a lark,' I say,
'I'd lift myself high up today.'
High up enough to see beyond,
My troubles waved with magic wand.

But in some very special way,
The lark's song calls us on.
It offers hope for each new day,
And teaches hearts how best to pray.

Not from selfish splendour,
Or for material gain.
But so our souls and minds can rest
From toil and from pain.

Oh little bird so brown and small,
You make my world feel ten feet tall.
I thrill just at the sight of you.
My heart joins yours,
My spirit soars,
If you can sing whilst on the wing,
Then I can tackle this day too!

Pitter, Patter, Play School

Pitter, patter, Peter,
Post, paste and potter.
Put poles in puddles proper,
Pam pushes pram to Peter.

Hot, heavy and healthy,
Peter pushed past Heather.
Pram held in sweaty hands,
Heather on hard dry ground stands.

Pitter, patter, Peter,
Prince, protective, proud.
Pouring pots of purple petals,
Over and around the crowd.

The Music Lives On

I'm sitting in the sunshine as the band begins to play,
There's music all around me on this momentous day.
Spring has woven webs of joy, as spiders come and go.
Birds are singing, bells are ringing,
Flowers budding now can show.

When I close my eyes and ponder,
What my life has brought.
My heart and head just wonder,
At the joy I once had sought.

Joy that now fills my days,
As a hymn that's filled with praise.
Joy that floats on wind and breeze,
Joy that rustles trees and leaves.

The music in my joyful song,
Was brought by you alone.
For here at last my soul can sing,
She's found her way back home.

Clothing the Shadows

Though often torn and tormented my outer self struggled on.
There were times the inner 'Wendy' felt completely dead and
    gone.
In order to resurrect her, 'Love' called and begged her to 'come'.
Wendy answered that sweet call that welcomed her back home.

The journey leading from darkness to dawn has taken me by
    the hand
Oft full of fear and unsure of the way, my feet have at last
    found firm ground.
Although a solitary traveller, I've shared with many a 'Highway'.
To mark the company of another gives light and can brighten
    the day.

The empty shadows so naked and plain that haunted my every
    step
Have retreated to their hiding place, their doubts have all been
    swept.
When I am tempted to look their way, I turn instead to hear
    another say,
'Wendy, walk with me today, leave those shadows, let's away.'

I need the prompt of another's hand, when I forget how to
    take my stand.
I value words of truth and light that help me find the way to
    fight.
I no longer walk in the shadows, I no longer feel estranged.
I've found my place: a true delight, a forest, ocean or mountain
    range.

For wherever my feet wonder now, I can sure footed be.
I no longer fear the shadows but welcome the chance to be
    free.
I can understand how shadows form and why they dance at
    night.
They need the light to help them show, but once in clothes
    they must go!
So, clothing the shadows is now my daily song.
I long for others to join this growing throng.

Don't let those empty shadows dictate who you are.
Instead, you lift your head up high,
Laugh loud at them, kiss them goodbye,
Goodbye, goodbye, goodbye.